CLASS 56 PICTOR

A hundred years from now railway historians will look back at the start of the 21st century and wonder just what happened to the class of locomotive known as the 56. With some examples not even 20 years old, the entire class was withdrawn from service en-bloc in April 2004.

Pretty much since the dawn of the railway, locomotives, coaches and wagons have run the course of their expected lives and when they became 'life expired' they retired to the scrap yard and new builds took over. That was how things had gone for 150 years until the start of the 21st century, when in the crazy world of privatisation, perfectly good locos and coaches, fully serviceable and only a third or a half of the way though their potential working lives were switched off and dumped in sidings, destined to decay and then be broken for scrap.

Of the men who designed and built the Class 56 locomotive in the 1970s and 1980s, who would have thought all 135 examples would have been withdrawn in 2004? A life expectancy of at least 30 years was surely in the design plan. Even in 1999, 114 locos were still in traffic. Six years later the Class 56 became history.

Having gained a cult following during their final years, the memories of this once 135-strong fleet live on for those who followed them to the bitter end. This second title from Train Crazy Publishing takes a look at the Class 56 locomotive. From the early days in BR blue through the multicoloured 1980s and 1990s, right through to the EWS years, more than 50 different locos are featured.

This book is a timely reminder of what really was a classic of loco classes - The Class 56.

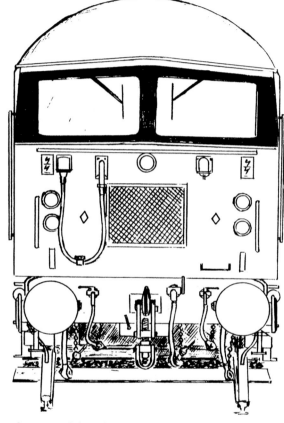

Outline drawing of the Class 56 loco from the British Rail Southern Region drivers manual. For a class of loco built essentially to haul coal trains to/from power stations, a number were allocated to the former Southern Region in the early 1990s for infrastructure duties.

First Published 2005
ISBN 0-9548035-2-3

Published by **Train Crazy Publishing**,
PO Box 13, South Shore, Blackpool. FY4 1TA.
Telephone and Fax: 01253 346005
Email: admin@tram-trainvideos.co.uk
Website: www.tram-trainvideos.co.uk

Printed in England.

~ ~ INTRODUCTION ~ ~

With the last major class of diesel locomotive (the Class 50) introduced in 1968, British Rail was looking for a new design, essentially a freight only machine, with neither vacuum brakes nor train heat supply, to cope with the increase in coal moved by rail to the various power stations in England, Scotland and Wales. The loco had to be big, powerful and able to haul heavy trains over long distances without the need for double heading, refuelling and/or loco changes.

Based on the successful Class 47 body shell and with a new engine design, tested in a Class 47, a 3250hp Co-Co locomotive was proposed. Ruston Paxman supplied the engine and together with a main alternator and traction motors from Brush, the Class 56 locomotive was born.

An initial order of 60 of these Type 5 machines were proposed but due to limitations at the various BR workshops, 30 of them were subcontracted to be built in Romania. The remaining 30 were built at Doncaster Works. As it turned out, an additional order for 75 locos meant a further 55 (85 in total) being built at Doncaster, with the last 20 being constructed at Crewe Works.

Having placed the order in 1974, it wasn't until August 1976 until the first two locos (56 001 and 56 002) arrived in Britain and following a whole series of modifications, it was February 1977 before the first Class 56 worked a revenue earning train. In the end, it took a staggering nine years, from when the framework for 56 001 was constructed in the Electroputere works in Craiova, Romania in late 1975 until Crewe rolled out the last machine, 56 135, in October 1984.

Although designed as a heavy freight loco, essentially hauling Merry-Go-Round coal hoppers, the sectorisation and subsequent privatisation of Britain's railways saw this design of loco stretched far and wide on a variety of freight duties. The only type of train these locos never hauled regularly was passenger coaches although they were always a popular choice for railtours, which again took them far and wide.

The aim of this book is to pay tribute to the Class 56 locomotive in photographic form during their 26 years on Britain's rail network. It is certainly not a history book and not every loco is featured but I've tried to include every major livery and livery variation.

From a personal point of view, I remember seeing these new big blue noisy freight locos in the early 1980s on spotting trips to Crewe during the school holidays. They always seemed 'hard' and 'big' compared to other classes. Perhaps it was that central headlight (on an almost headlight-free railway) or maybe it was that odd looking grid dead centre in the front. Another treat was a ride behind one on the test train from Crewe to Holyhead. I remember 56 135 on its debut. The last built and the first in Railfreight livery. Ah, the memories!

Acknowledgements: I would like to thank the following people for their help with this book: Jason Prescott, Mary Meskell, Elizabeth Meskell, Travel Lens Photographic, Jim Ramsay, Ken White, Andy Harkness, Justin Perkins and Alvin Nathaniel Joiner.

Enjoy the book

Nick Meskell

Early Class 56 namings used the standard BR nameplate of the day with lower case silver letters on a red background with silver border. Plates were affixed centrally to both sides of the loco body, normally just above the BR double arrow symbol. 56 040 received these plates at Swansea station in March 1982. *(Nick Meskell collection)*

To provide some background information on the Class 56 I've chosen five years over a 20 year period between 1984 and 2004 to provide an at-a-glance guide to the status of the 135 locomotives. As you will see, 1984 was plain and simple; by 2004 so many liveries, sectors, pools, namings, allocations, reallocations etc., had come and gone......

On 1st January 1984 Crewe Works were finishing off the last seven locos of the 20 built there. 56 128 had been accepted into traffic shortly before Christmas 1983 and 56 129 was undergoing final testing. Work was underway on the final loco, 56 135, which made an official entry into service in October.

The 128 locos in service on the first day of 1984 were allocated to five depots: Bristol Bath Road, Cardiff Canton, Gateshead, Tinsley and Toton. Later in the year Gateshead received five brand new locos in the shape of 56 130 to 56 134 and Tinsley bagged the last one.

There were two liveries at the time: all over blue (latterly known as BR Blue) and Large Logo blue. From new, the first 35 locos were painted in the standard rail blue of the day. 56 036 was chosen to test the Large Logo design and although successful, 56 037 to 56 083 continued to be outshopped in plain blue. From 56 084 (in 1980) the Large Logo became standard and the remainder of the class were finished in this style (except 56 135 which was the first loco in the grey Railfreight livery).

In 1984 the naming of diesel locos wasn't particularly common, although nine Class 56s had received names: 56 031, 56 032, 56 035, 56 037, 56 038, 56 040, 56 074, 56 076 and 56 124. The first naming was of Cardiff based 56 038 which received 'Western Mail' in June 1981 at Cardiff Central station. Oddly, being designed for heavy freight, in particular coal, the choice of this type of loco for a 'mail' theme was certainly strange! 56 111 ran with the unofficial name 'Nelson' for a short while in 1983.

GRID NUMBER CRUNCH: 1/1/84

Based at Cardiff Canton	9
Based at Bristol Bath Road	11
Based at Gateshead	4
Based at Tinsley	78
Based at Toton	26
Under Construction at Crewe Works	7
Total	**135**

Sectorisation was all the rage in the late 1980s and by the 1st January 1989, the Class 56 was preparing itself for the run up to privatisation with five operating sectors. By this time Gateshead, Tinsley and Bristol had all lost their allocations with Toton becoming the main depot, housing more than 100 locos.

The five operating pools were as follows:
FAWC - Freight (Aggregates) - Cardiff Canton
FALX - Freight (Aggregates) - Leicester Area (Based at Toton)
FENB - Freight (Power Station Coal) - Nottinghamshire (Based at Toton)
FEYA - Freight (Power Station Coal) - Yorkshire (Based at Toton)
FEYB - Freight (Power Station Coal) - North East (Based at Toton)

(If you think this was silly, worse was yet to come, but why Power Station Coal? Why specify Power Station? Well, at this time, even the type of coal carried by rail was subject to sectorisation: Power Station Coal, General Coal and Coal Distribution!).

Five different liveries were carried: Blue, Large Logo, Railfreight, Railfreight Red Stripe and the New Railfreight livery of two or three tone grey with sub-sector markings. The majority of low numbered locos sported the new grey livery while Large Logo was still carried by the high numbers.

22 'Grids' carried names on 1st January 1989: 56 001, 56 028, 56 031, 56 032, 56 034, 56 035, 56 037, 56 038, 56 040, 56 053, 56 063, 56 074, 56 075, 56 095, 56 122, 56 123, 56 124, 56 131, 56 132, 56 133, 56 134 and 56 135. The majority of names were themed with locations that Class 56 locos worked to or the type of trains they hauled, such as 56 028 - 'West Burton Power Station', 56 074 - 'Kellingley Colliery', 56 123 - 'Drax Power Station' and 56 124 - 'Blue Circle Cement'. The last five locos constructed were all named. 56 133 became 'Crewe Locomotive Works' at the open day held there in June 1984. First built 56 001 was named 'Whatley' at Whatley Quarry in October 1987.

GRID NUMBER CRUNCH: 1/1/89

FAWC pool - Based at Cardiff Canton	26
FALX pool - Based at Toton	11
FENB pool - Based at Toton	27
FEYA pool - Based at Toton	47
FEYB pool - Based at Toton	24
Total	**135**

Another early naming for the class was carried out on 56 031 at Merehead Quarry in September 1993. Based at Bristol at the time, this loco then moved to Cardiff, Stewarts Lane, Toton, Stewarts Lane (again), Toton (again), then Immingham and finally to Thornaby where the nameplates were removed in May 1996. *(Nick Meskell collection)*

~ ~ GRID STATS: 1994 ~ ~

From sectorisation came the last hurdle before full privatisation and like many classes of loco the Class 56 had been divided, sub-divided and split in all directions. Looking back now, what a load of mumbo jumbo it was, but at the time it must have meant something to somebody! The once common sight of a Class 56 hauled coal train was less common, with locos split far and wide including a small number allocated to Network SouthEast for infrastructure duties.

21 locos were withdrawn from service or put into store in the 1989-1993 period. 56 002 suffered severe damage following derailment near Blyth Bridge while working a coal train in June 1991. The loco never ran again and was stripped for spares. 56 017 was withdrawn from service following a collision with 31 549 at Ashby-de-la-Zouch in November 1991. 56 023 caught fire near Ambergate in November 1989 while working an empty MGR train and although repaired, only lasted a few more years before going into store. 56 122 was only eight years old when it ran through the buffers at Ryhope Grange Junction, also in November 1991. The loco suffered severe damage after its train followed on and three MGR hoppers smashed into it. The other 17 locos out of traffic at this time were: 56 001, 56 008, 56 012, 56 013, 56 014, 56 015, 56 016, 56 020, 56 022, 56 024, 56 026, 56 027, 56 028, 56 030, 56 042, 56 052 and 56 066.

On the 1st January 1994 there were sixteen pools, of which 12 were operating pools for the 126 serviceable locos and they were based at five depots: Cardiff, Immingham, Thornaby, Toton and Stewarts Lane. The 12 operating pools were:

FASB - Trainload Construction - Based at Stewarts Lane
FCBN - Trainload Coal (East Midlands) - Based at Toton
FCCI - Trainload Coal - Based at Immingham
FCDN - Trainload Coal (Yorkshire) - Based at Toton
FCEN - Trainload Coal (North East) - Based at Toton
FCKK - Trainload Coal - Based at Cardiff
FCNN - Trainload Coal (North West) - Based at Toton
FCPA - Trainload Coal and Petroleum (Scotland) - Based at Toton
FMCK - Trainload Metals - Based at Cardiff
FMTY - Trainload Metals - Based at Thornaby
FPGI - Trainload Petroleum - Based at Immingham
NKJM - Network SE Infrastructure (Meldon Quarry) - Based at Stewarts Lane

There were eight different liveries to be seen on these locos in 1994: BR Blue, Railfreight and Railfreight Red Stripe survived from the BR days. (All the Large Logo examples had been repainted). Civil Engineers grey and yellow livery was new and carried by six locos, whilst the majority wore the grey livery with either no sub-sector branding or Coal, Metals or Construction branding.

A credible 39 locos carried nameplates in 1994. Some of the newcomers were: 56 044 - 'Cardiff Canton' (named 8/91); 56 069 - 'Thornaby TMD' (6/93) and 56 110 - 'Croft' (9/92). The full list of named locos was: 56 001, 56 031, 56 032, 56 034, 56 037, 56 038, 56 040, 56 044, 56 051, 56 053, 56 054, 56 060, 56 062, 56 063, 56 069, 56 073, 56 074, 56 075, 56 076, 56 077, 56 080, 56 089, 56 091, 56 093, 56 094, 56 095, 56 099, 56 101, 56 102, 56 110, 56 114, 56 117, 56 123, 56 128, 56 130, 56 131, 56 133, 56 134 and 56 135.

Another point worth making is that by 1st January 1994, six locos had been de-rated. Built with a 3250hp engine, 56 069, 56 077 and 56 107 had all been de-rated to 2400hp whilst 56 083, 56 084 and 56 086 were down to 2800hp.

GRID NUMBER CRUNCH: 1/1/94

FASB pool - Based at Stewarts Lane	14
FCBN pool - Based at Toton	4
FCCI pool - Based at Immingham	5
FCDN pool - Based at Toton	25
FCEN pool - Based at Toton	16
FCKK pool - Based at Cardiff	4
FCNN pool - Based at Toton	6
FCPA pool - Based at Toton	9
FMCK pool - Based at Cardiff	10
FMTY pool - Based at Thornaby	11
FPGI pool - Based at Immingham	4
NKJM pool - Based at Stewarts Lane	6
Stored or Withdrawn	21
Total	**135**

By 1st January 1999 it was almost like the good old BR days for the Class 56 locomotives. All the silly operating pools and codes had gone, the locos were based at one depot and could work any train to any part of the country and a start had been made on painting all locos in the same livery! However, in the interim 1994-1998 period, there had been more twists and turns with the locos abandoning the coal, metals and infrastructure pools to fall into the Transrail and Load Haul operating companies. Following this, all survivors were sold en-bloc to Wisconsin Central in February 1996 and came under the control of the newly formed English Welsh & Scottish Railway (EWS). Looking back, what a waste of time all the sectorisation and pooling turned out to be, although from a loco livery point of view, we got the highly acclaimed orange and black Load Haul livery before the maroon and gold of EWS ended the livery story.

Of the 135 locos built, 13 were scrapped and one was transferred to Departmental use in the 1994-1998 period. A further seven locos were stored or withdrawn. This gave a total of 114 machines in service on the first day of 1999. 56 002 was scrapped first, cut up at Doncaster in March 1994. 56 017 and 56 042 were also scrapped in 1994. None were scrapped in 1995, but in 1996 a further four were broken: 56 005, 56 015, 56 024 and 56 026. 56 005 had sustained severe fire damage. Tragically in 1997, pioneer member 56 001 was cut along with 56 016 then in 1998, 56 020, 56 028, 56 030 and the baby of the fleet, 56 122 all met their maker. 56 009 was withdrawn from service in 1996 and moved to Brush Traction at Loughborough to be used to test overhauled power units and engines. Entering the premises as 56 009, the loco was unnumbered for a while, before being allocated 56 201 in December 1998. Unlike classes like 37, 47 and 86, a Class 56 had never carried any other fleet number than the TOPS number allocated from new. To date 56 009 is the first, last and only! The seven locos stored or withdrawn on the first day of 1999 were 56 008, 56 012, 56 013, 56 014, 56 023, 56 038 and 56 110.

Compared to 1994, operating pools and allocations couldn't have been easier. All 114 operational locos were in the WGAN pool (which stood for EWS Class 56!) and all were based at Immingham!

Despite the blanket EWS ownership and operation, the surviving locos carried a staggering nine different liveries between them. In fact there were actually more than this, discounting minor variations such as the EWS or EW&S lettering and many throwbacks to the days of BR (like BR double arrow symbols on Transrail branded Civil Engineers 'Dutch' colours!). Remarkably one loco 56 004 remained in BR Blue while another single loco - 56 019 - was in the Railfreight Red Stripe livery. The other seven recognised colour schemes were: Load Haul, Railfreight Coal, Railfreight Metals, EWS (or EW&S), Civil Engineers, Transrail (big 'T' on two tone grey bodyside) and Civil Engineers Transrail (big 'T' on yellow/grey).

The name game was still thriving in 1999 with 34 locos carrying nameplates. 56 103 was named 'STORA' in July 1997 and a number of locos were renamed or had their plates transferred. 56 089 was named 'Ferrybridge C Power Station' in September 1991 and carried these plates until January 1995. A month later the plates were affixed to a gleaming 56 006 in Load Haul livery. (See page 42). 56 091 was originally to be named 'The Institute of Mining Engineers' but ended up with 'Castle Donington Power Station' in 1989 and then 'Stanton' in 1998. The 34 named locos on 1/1/99 were: 56 006, 56 033, 56 034, 56 038, 56 040, 56 044, 56 045, 56 050, 56 052, 56 053, 56 054, 56 057, 56 063, 56 069, 56 073, 56 074, 56 075, 56 077, 56 080, 56 086, 56 087, 56 091, 56 094, 56 099, 56 101, 56 103, 56 110, 56 112, 56 123, 56 130, 56 131, 56 133, 56 134 and 56 135.

GRID NUMBER CRUNCH: 1/1/99

WGAN pool - Based at Immingham	114
Stored or Withdrawn	7
Departmental	1
Scrapped	13
Total	**135**

~ ~ GRID STATS: 2004 ~ ~

In all fairness to EWS, when they took over freight operations in Britain in 1996, they inherited a motley bunch of locomotives in various states of disrepair. It was only common sense to replace what were almost 40 year old life expired classes like 31s, 33s, 37s, 47s and 86s. Love them or hate them, these locos really were past their best and a new class was needed. For the Class 56 and the 58s, 60s, 90s and 92s as well, there was no need for replacement. In particular the Class 56 with the oldest member only 20 years old - just over half way through its expected life - and the newest member - a mere 12 years old, there was certainly nothing wrong with these locos and they were a big part of the EWS plan. However, eight years later and the history is now written. The introduction of 250 brand new Class 66 locos, improved diagramming, the loss of the Royal Mail contract and other freight flows, resulted in a catastrophic change which saw the complete withdrawal of all EWS owned Class 31s, 33s, 47s, 86s and even the 'as new' Class 58s. Class 60s, 90s and 92s are all now in store and for the Class 56 - it all ended on 31st March 2004.

Prior to that day, during the period covered here (1999 to 2003), the Class 56s were subject to various withdrawals, reinstatements and the reintroduction of numerous operating or as it reads 'non-operating' pools. In that five year period, the class tumbled from a respectable 114 serviceable locos to a pitiful 24. Ninety locos were wiped off the books with the majority of disused machines dumped at various sidings and depots around the country. A few were sold off and more were scrapped.

On the first day of their final year (1/1/04), the Class 56 locos were split into six pools of which only one was actually operational. There was some method in the madness, as at least EWS had a withdrawal/reinstatement policy. The six pools were:

SDXL - Fragonset Railways - Stored locomotives
WGAI - EWS Class 56 - Based at Immingham
WNSS - EWS main line locos - Stored serviceable
WNTR - EWS main line locos - Tactical reserve
WNXX - EWS main line locos - Stored unserviceable
WNZX - EWS main line locos - Awaiting disposal
(Other than locos in the WGAI pool, allocations for the stored pools were random - basically where the loco was stabled/dumped. This includes the Fragonset locos).

As on 1st January 2004, a total of 25 locos had been scrapped with another three in Departmental use or sold privately. With 13 locos cut between 1994 and 1998, a further 12 were broken between 1999 and the end of 2003. These were: 56 126 (in 1999), 56 008, 56 012, 56 014 and 56 035 (in 2000), 56 013 and 56 092 (in 2001) and 56 019, 56 047, 56 080, 56 123 and the last loco built, 56 135 (in 2003).

Quite a number of 56s received the EWS maroon and gold livery and had this company continued with the operation of the class, all examples may well have ended up in these colours. As it turned out, repaints stopped when the class went into terminal decline. Thanks to the pressure and sponsorship of enthusiast groups, two retro liveries were reborn when 56 006 went from Load Haul orange into a stunning coat of BR blue in August 1999 (losing its nameplates at the same time) while the cover loco - 56 078 - was actually in EWS colours when it returned to the magical Large Logo livery of the mid- 1980s. Other liveries in 2004 included EWS, Civil Engineers, Load Haul and grey with either a big 'T' or the former Metals and Coal sub-sector branding.

When a class is in decline, it's not normal practice to name them and in fact more locos lost their nameplates than gained new ones. Only 20 examples carried nameplates at the end. Two new ones worth noting were on 56 078 which as well as receiving Large Logo livery, gained the name 'Doncaster Enterprise' at Toton depot in October 2003. EWS liveried machine 56 115 was named 'Barry Needham' at Doncaster Royal Mail Terminal in February 2002. Mr. Needham, who was an EWS coal train controller, was killed in the Great Heck crash in February 2001. Ironically, this loco was the last of its kind to be built at Doncaster and was paired with 'Doncaster Enterprise' on the farewell train on 31st March 2004. For the record the full 20 named Grids on 1/1/04 were: 56 033, 56 038, 56 045, 56 050, 56 054, 56 057, 56 069, 56 073, 56 078, 56 086, 56 087, 56 091, 56 094, 56 101, 56 103, 56 110, 56 112, 56 115, 56 131 and 56 134. Worth noting is that from this list, only five of these locos were actual runners at the time.

GRID NUMBER CRUNCH: 1/1/04

SDXL pool - Fragonset owned	3
WGAI pool - Based at Immingham	24
Stored or Withdrawn	80
Departmental	1
Sold/Preserved	2
Scrapped	25
Total	**135**

LIVERY TRIVIA
Between 1977 and 2004 - excluding oddities (like 56 073 on page 41) - Class 56 locomotives carried 15 different liveries: BR Blue, Large Logo blue, Railfreight, Railfreight Red Stripe, grey with Coal branding, grey with Metals branding, grey with Distribution branding, grey with Petroleum branding, grey with Transrail branding, Civil Engineers, Civil Engineers with Transrail branding, Load Haul and EWS.

NAME TRIVIA
A total of 59 locos were named: 56 001, 56 006, 56 012, 56 028, 56 030, 56 031, 56 032, 56 033, 56 034, 56 035, 56 037, 56 038, 56 039, 56 040, 56 044, 56 045, 56 050, 56 051, 56 052, 56 053, 56 054, 56 057, 56 060, 56 062, 56 063, 56 069, 56 073, 56 074, 56 075, 56 076, 56 077, 56 078, 56 080, 56 086, 56 087, 56 089, 56 091, 56 093, 56 094, 56 095, 56 099, 56 101, 56 102, 56 103, 56 110, 56 112, 56 114, 56 115, 56 117, 56 122, 56 123, 56 124, 56 128, 56 130, 56 131, 56 132, 56 133, 56 134 and 56 135.

2004 INTO 2005
Although the aim of this book is to cover the Class 56 story up until final withdrawal in April 2004, for the sake of completeness, it is worth looking at the period between April 2004 and the completion date of this book in February 2005. In this ten month period, three lucky locos passed into preservation and nine have been exported to France for use on the construction of a new railway line. More are expected to follow. As at 21st February 2005, 56 038, 56 059, 56 060, 56 069, 56 078, 56 087, 56 090, 56117 and 56118 were all working for Fertis in France. (Note 56 078 - minus its nameplates and in Large Logo livery!).
The three preserved locos are:
56 003 - Load Haul livery; privately owned; located at MOD Ashchurch; under restoration.
56 057 - in EWS livery (named 'British Fuels'); privately owned; located at Nene Valley Railway; operational.
56 097 - in grey livery with Trainload Metals branding; privately owned; located at Brush Traction, Loughborough; under restoration.
Four further locos, 56 045, 56 061, 56 066 and 56 124 are currently in the WNSO pool. These have been sold and are awaiting collection.

The BR Blue Years

Wooden scotches under the centre wheels of the front bogie indicate that all is not well with 56 020 in this 28th December 1993 shot at Toton. Having been delivered in February 1977 and entered service in May 1977, 56 020 ran for 15 years until going into store in September 1992. The loco was cut six years later. Unlike the majority of other 56s, this loco only ever carried the BR blue livery. Snowplough-fitted 20 135 behind, also destined for the scrapman, managed to escape and remarkably still survives in storage under the ownership of Direct Rail Services. *(Nick Meskell collection)*

All 30 Romanian-built locos arrived in Britain via Harwich between August 1976 and August 1977. 56 028 and 56 029 came in together in July 1977 and as per their sisters, were immediately put into store pending modifications. 56 029 entered service in September 1977 but missed a full 12 month period between November 1978 and 1979 following a collision. With slight front end damage here, 56 029 is stabled at Tinsley in this 21st March 1987 photograph. In 1988, the loco received the new two tone grey livery with Trainload Coal branding. *(Nick Meskell collection)*

If you had to choose one photograph to describe exactly what the 56 was and what it did in the late 1970s and into the 1980s, then this would be it: Blue loco with HAA coal hoppers, working to/from Power Stations, all day every day, over and over and over again. In fact, you may well have been bored with this scene but that was exactly what the Class 56 was built to do and it's a job they did exceptionally well. 56 081 with large end numbers picks its way across the pointwork at Doncaster station with a lengthy but empty rake of hoppers on 23rd August 1988. This loco managed nine years in BR blue before going grey. It eventually ended up in EWS livery. (See page 51).
(Nick Meskell collection)

A lovely shot of 56 042 on a lengthy train of Redland stone hoppers taken from the tall over bridge at Wellingborough on 19th July 1985. As well as the colourful selection of period cars in the car park, the station still boasted platforms on the slow lines although they look disused. Pride of place is the station signal box, in the centre (where else?) and of course the semaphore signals. At the top left, you may just be able to see the junction signal box. Although looking smart in a coat of newly applied blue, 56 042 had a tragically short life, suffering fire damage in 1983, then a period of disuse between April 1986 and June 1987 before being taken out of service for good in December 1989 - being only TEN years old! The end result was quite nasty. (See page 56). *(Nick Meskell collection)*

56 068 glides past the camera at Westbury on 19th June 1986. As the 28th Class 56 built at Doncaster, the loco started life in BR blue before receiving a coat of Railfreight Red Stripe. In 1991 the loco received the new grey livery with Coal brandings. In 1996 the loco went all white prior to the introduction of the new EW&S maroon and gold which it received in due course. *(Nick Meskell collection)*

With an incredible 43 fully laden (and they really are fully laden!) coal hoppers in tow, 56 057 passes Finedon Road signal box with a southbound train on 23rd September 1981. This is another fantastic railway scene with semaphore signals, dozens of sidings and a Class 25 busy in the yard. In this photo, 56 057 was just over two years old. The loco was named 'British Fuels' in June 1996. Unlike many other locos featured in this book, 56 057 is now safe and sound, based at the Nene Valley Railway and became the first of its class to work in preservation in 2004. *(Nick Meskell collection)*

Looking at the history of loco classes like 37, 47 and 86, it's incredible to see how many of them were renumbered, then renumbered again, then rebuilt, gaining many different liveries and even names along the way. A number of Class 56s went through the rainbow of liveries as well but 56 004 was the complete opposite. It started life in blue numbered 56 004 and it finished life in blue as 56 004. In fact, with a few exceptions - such as modern headlight, orange stripe and no BR logo - this 1996 photo could be 1986, or even 1976! The reason for this may well have been as a result of a head-on collision with two Class 31s in July 1982. The resulting severe damage saw 56 004 out of service until June 1984, although after repairs at Doncaster Works it really should have gone into at least Large Logo livery as per the last built 'Grid' constructed at this location (56 115) in late 1982. Today 56 004 awaits the cutter's torch at Wigan. In the photo the loco is stabled at Warrington Arpley on 5th October 1996.
(Nick Meskell collection)

The Large Logo Years

Brand new, fresh from the box, 56 111 stands in all its glory at Doncaster Works in October 1982. At this time, the final four locos built here were almost complete and work was well underway on the construction of the Class 58s. When it comes to livery descriptions, nobody really counted the colour of the roof until the terminology 'triple grey' came along to describe the Railfreight livery of the late 1980s. Technically speaking, if you count the roof colour, the Large Logo livery was almost as much grey as it was blue as well as yellow, white and black! 56 111 was back at Doncaster for a repaint into Load Haul livery 13 years after this photo was taken! *(Travel Lens Photographic)*

Another photo taken at Shirebrook on 20th July 1985 with an equally impressive line up of Large Logo 56s. At least five examples are here, headed by 56 105 on the left. The end number on this loco has a very 'home made' look to it. (Man in glove scrapes grease off buffer and writes number!). During its lifetime, this loco was based at Tinsley, Toton, Stewarts Lane, Cardiff, Immingham and Thornaby. Presently dumped at Toton, 56 105 is earmarked for a move to France in 2005. *(Nick Meskell collection)*

56 130, complete with white bodyside grill, looks very smart in this undated photograph. The loco was named 'Wardley Opencast' at the site of the Wardley Opencast mine near Newcastle in November 1990. Outshopped from Crewe in April 1984, the loco would have taken a trip to Holyhead on the morning test train prior to entering service. In December 1994 the loco was painted into Load Haul livery at Doncaster. It was the highest numbered Class 56 in this livery. Ten years later the loco was broken by C F Booth of Rotherham. *(Ken White)*

A work-stained 56 120 shares the sidings at Immingham with a pair of 37s and a 31 on a snowy December afternoon in 1986. From new in May 1983, this loco was based at Tinsley before a move to Gateshead in 1986 and then Toton, Immingham, Thornaby, Immingham (2nd time), Thornaby (2nd time) and finally Immingham for the third time in 1996. Compare this to 56 040 (page 25), for example, which spent 18 years at the same depot! *(Travel Lens Photographic)*

56 048 is caught on camera running light engine on to Bristol Bath Road on 17th June 1986. This was one of three locos which were completed in the standard blue livery and were subsequently repainted into Large Logo at Landore depot in Swansea. (047 and 049 were the other two). A year after this picture was taken 56 048 was in the Railfreight Red Stripe livery and in 1993 the loco went into the yellow and grey Civil Engineers colours. Remarkably, given the various possible Trainload branding, Transrail, Loadhaul or EWS, the loco finished its days in yellow and grey. The loco is presently awaiting scrapping at Immingham. *(Nick Meskell collection)*

The Railfreight Years

Upon completion at Crewe in October 1984, 56 135 became the first of the class to be painted into the new Railfreight livery. For all intents and purposes, it was the same as Large Logo with grey replacing blue as the main bodyside colour. At the time, 56 135 had the huge BR arrows painted dead centre on the loco body. Subsequent repaints saw the arrows off-set as per 56 036 in this photo (and like 56 048 opposite). Departing Severn Tunnel Junction with an eastbound oil tanker train on 20th June 1986, 56 036 - painted in December 1985 - was one of six locos painted in this livery at Landore. Note the motley collection of cars in the staff car park, in particular the brown Reliant Robin. What a colour! There are just not enough brown cars on the roads these days! *(Nick Meskell collection)*

A freshly painted 56 077 stands in the works at Doncaster in February 1986. Having been built here in early 1980 and painted in blue at the time, this loco was back for yet another colour scheme - Load Haul - in December 1994. Having led such mundane lives it is quite hard to find a 'claim to fame' for the 56s (compared to say Deltics, Westerns or even 37s and 47s) but 56 077 - when only one month old - was chosen to represent its type at the Rainhill 150 event in June 1980. Not only did it do that, but it towed the APT through the procession! On another occasion this loco received a round of applause when the curtain was pulled back to reveal the name 'Thorpe Marsh Power Station' at that location in a ceremony held in September 1990. *(Ken White)*

There's a real summer feel to this undated shot (1988?) of 56 075 stabled at Knottingley Depot. One of the rare occasions when a Class 56 locomotive naming ceremony took place in a main line station occurred at Leeds on 9th July 1985 when this loco was named 'West Yorkshire Enterprise'. Looking at the position of the nameplates, it's fairly obvious the central location above the BR arrows of blue livery was chosen. The use of cab end numbers was fairly uncommon at this time although it seems the 075 here is made up of proper transfers rather than the more usual greasy finger technique described earlier. *(Travel Lens Photographic)*

56 041 was a real South Wales machine, spending 12 years of its life (August 1979 to September 1991) based at Cardiff Canton. As-far-as-the-eye-can-see coal trains were very much the norm as the loco passes its home depot heading westbound empties on 25th June 1986. Other liveries carried by this loco were blue, grey with Trainload Construction branding and finally EWS. *(Nick Meskell collection)*

A lovely crisp shot of 56 040 'Oystermouth' at Bristol Bath Road Depot. This loco was the last to be painted into this type of Railfreight livery at Crewe in March 1987. This was another loco with a long history in South Wales. Moving from Toton to Cardiff in September 1979, the loco spent 18 years working off Canton Depot before a final move in September 1997 to Immingham where it was subsequently stored.
(Travel Lens Photographic)

Following the drab grey Railfreight livery came a revised style known simply as Railfreight Red Stripe. Initially designed for locos that had a natural solebar like 20s and 58s, the red stripe was soon added to many classes - 56s included. This is 56 067 pictured near Chesterfield with a southbound train of empty MGR hoppers on 25th July 1988. The red stripe is fairly obvious, the smaller BR arrows (compared to the Large Logo livery) were perhaps not. This loco, now in EWS livery, is stored out of use at Ferrybridge. *(Nick Meskell collection)*

The 'Grey' Years

Jumping out of sequence slightly and before moving into the desperately unimaginative and uninspiring world of the grey livery with various brandings, here are three locos in the double grey (or triple grey) without any branding. First is 56 123 receiving attention at Doncaster Works on 12th July 1992, obviously freshly painted and sporting a silver on black power station diamond. This silver/black theme extended to the loco nameplates as well. This loco was named 'Drax Power Station' in May 1988. Looking at the photo, the superb condition of the loco and the fact it was only nine years old at the time, it is difficult to understand the railway policy in Britain which dictated that only SEVEN years after the photo was taken the loco was put into store and then FOUR after this (in 2003), it was scrapped. Was it really that bad? *(Nick Meskell collection)*

It is often debated by enthusiasts as to whether this livery was two-tone grey or triple grey. If you look at the body sides there are clearly only two shades of grey but if you count the roof as well, there are three. However, when did roof colours ever come into livery descriptions? Were those Stratford 31s and 47s blue and silver livery? And was Regional Railways livery white, grey, dark blue, light blue and… black? Whether double or triple, here is a freshly painted 56 082 - complete with BR arrows - at Immingham on 14th March 1994. 56 098 in matching livery stands behind. Note the difference in headlight position and grid design on the fronts of 003 and 082. *(Nick Meskell collection)*

All is quiet after a light dusting of snow at Toton on 28th December 1993 with unbranded 56 108 in front of another unbranded machine. Once again the paint job appears to be ex-works. Initially based at Healey Mills, then Tinsley, 56 108 had been a Toton loco since January 1987 and spent 11 months out of service at this depot between March 1990 and February 1991. Exactly ten years after this photo was taken 56 108 was withdrawn from service. *(Nick Meskell collection)*

Just Another 'Grid' Day

56 079 and 56 110 head an impressive line-up of locos on Knottingley Depot in this undated photo. It is hoped we have a centre spread of locos resting between duties on a Sunday afternoon in summer although problems of drivers taking industrial action or general problems within the coal industry may paint a different picture. Nevertheless, an incredible line-up of at least 14 locos can be seen here - it could be as many as 20 or 25 if the roads to the right are four or five locos deep. Of the visible locos, BR blue and Railfreight dominate with just a couple of Large Logo examples. *(Travel Lens Photographic)*

Moving into the world of grey with the Trainload branding first introduced in 1987. Prior to receiving this livery, 56 084s claim to fame was being the first Class 56 painted in the Large Logo livery (in November 1980), after the livery had been tried out on 56 036. A further 31 locos were painted in this style at Doncaster with 19 of the Crewe built machines following. In the photo the loco stands deep in HAA territory at Scunthorpe on 5th June 1994. In April 1995, the loco went into Load Haul and was withdrawn in 2000. *(Nick Meskell collection)*

56 009 and 58 002 stand side by side at Leicester on 5th May 1996. (56 009 was actually 'stored' at this time). As mentioned in the introduction, 56 009 is the only member (so far) to have been renumbered, although as 56 201, the loco will never see the light of day. In the photo, 56 009 is just another Class 56 in the Coal branding, complete with the additional black diamonds on yellow strip next to the cab door. New in May 1977, this loco ran for 19 years until withdrawal in August 1996. After a postponed trip to Booth Roe for scrapping, the loco instead went to Brush Works in Loughborough to be used for spares and is now a test bed. *(Nick Meskell collection)*

The third loco shown in the Coal branding is 56 134 'Blyth Power', stabled at Crewe on 18th October 1997. (56 110 is behind). Second to last off the production line at Crewe, this loco was of course the last into Large Logo livery from new - this, in September 1984 and in October 1986 it was named. It would appear that prior to withdrawal in 2002, Large Logo and Trainload Coal were the only two liveries carried by this machine. 56 134 is one of 34 Class 56s currently dumped at Immingham. *(Nick Meskell collection)*

When the Class 56 was first introduced, a trip to Springs Branch Depot in Wigan would have entailed a new headlight bulb, some other minor maintenance or most likely a tank full of fuel. Today of course, 'SP' has lost its allocation of locos and moved on from being a TMD and stabling point. Very few locos that enter the premises come out intact. Hell on earth for the old diesel. In this particular photo, taken on 2nd May 1994, the Trainload Metals branded 56 054 was 'just visiting' and lived to fight another day. Named 'British Steel Llanwern' in May 1993, this loco ran for nine more years and still wearing the same livery as shown here, the loco currently resides at Ferrybridge. *(Nick Meskell collection)*

A March 1991 dated shot of 56 070 at Hither Green Depot. The loco wears a clean coat of grey with the Construction branding. Note the additional yellow and blue strip near the cab door. 56 070 was one of 14 locos based at Stewarts Lane in the mid 1990s in this livery. Unlike the six earmarked for Civils, these 14 were in the FASB pool, designated for construction duties in the South East. This loco eventually fell under the Transrail spell and finished its days in February 2004 in the big 'T' grey livery. *(Nick Meskell collection)*

56 031 was the first Class 56 built in Britain, and emerged from Doncaster Works on the Broughton Lane to Peterborough test train in May 1977. After stints at Toton, Tinsley, Healey Mills, Bristol and Cardiff, this loco moved to Stewarts Lane in September 1991. This only lasted a short while and this Trainload Coal liveried loco was back at Toton by March of 1992. In November 1992 the loco moved back south and enjoyed a two year stay at Stewarts Lane, gaining the 'Dutch' livery and surprisingly, retaining the name 'Merehead' (applied while based at Bristol in 1983). In the photo 56 031 stands at Worksop at dusk on 10th March 2000 with the scars of the BR arrows and nameplates, so cruelly wrenched from the loco bodyside. *(Nick Meskell collection)*

In 1993 six locomotives were painted into Civil Engineers livery and allocated to Stewarts Lane Depot in London in the NKJM pool. For 56 048 this was a real culture change, having been based at Toton from new and then Cardiff and Bristol. From heavy coal trains in South Wales, this loco found itself deep in third rail country with new work to and from Meldon Quarry. The loco spent exactly one year allocated here. In the photo 56 048 is stabled at Immingham ten days after the date was painted on the front wheel of each bogie - 18/1/95! *(Nick Meskell collection)*

Left: 56 036 is another loco which has carried a rainbow of liveries. Used as the test bed for the Large Logo livery in 1978 it then went on to be painted in Railfreight livery at Landore in December 1985 (page 21). Next, in 1989, came the grey livery with Trainload branding and of the four types of branding applied to Class 56s, only 036 received the blue and yellow wave design, known as Petroleum. In 1992, the loco went south where it became yellow and grey. Shown in this livery, a clean looking 56 036 is stabled on Warrington Arpley on 30th May 1994. A further livery variation came when a big 'T' was added to the bodyside prior to withdrawal in January 2000.
(Nick Meskell collection)

Right: To complete the 'Dutch' pages, here is 56 046 stabled at Stewarts Lane Depot on 16th May 1993. Having been based here since January 1993, the paint job certainly looks fresh. The letters NKJM actually stood for Network SouthEast Infrastructure and although clearly designated for Civil Engineers duties, how sweet would it have been if some of these locos had made it into the famed Network SouthEast livery!
(Nick Meskell collection)

The Transrail Years

56 133

Crewe Locomotive Works

TRANSRAIL

After many years of sectors, sub-sectors, pools and liveries, the final hurdle before 'real' privatisation came in 1994 when the freight business in the UK was split into three companies: Mainline, Transrail and Load Haul. Sadly, no Class 56 locos were allocated to Mainline, thus depriving us of repaints into their attractive 'aircraft' blue livery. For the 56s then, it was Transrail - who opted not to have a livery, and Load Haul - who went all out in colour and design. We start with 56 133 in the former grey livery with a big 'T'. Hidden in the dirt under the bodyside grill is the wording for this company. In this May 1996 shot, not only did this loco still retain its original nameplates, but they remained in the original red and silver. 56 133 (and 60 061 in 'clean' Transrail!) are at Ellesmere Port. *(Nick Meskell collection)*

Left: 56 073 at Scunthorpe on 5th May 1997. This is a virtually identical shot to 56 133 opposite, but an awful lot cleaner, without the BR arrows and with the black and silver nameplate. The loco was named 'Tremorfa Steelworks' at Doncaster as late as March 1993. *(Nick Meskell collection)*

Right: Here is another image of 56 073, this time at Rotherham, exactly a year after the one above. Following a graffiti attack the lower bodyside has been cleaned, which has allowed the chevrons of the Trainload Metals branding to reappear, giving a unique Transrail Metals livery! Just for fun, 56 073 is: two/three tone grey with full yellow front ends, black windscreen surrounds, blue and yellow bodyside branding with additional large white 'T' on a blue background with white inner circle, red outer circle and two red stripes underneath with an additional vertical red stripe at the cab end; the letters TRANSRAIL in white capitals and a black and silver nameplate with a blue and red crest above! (Try to fit that one in your notebook!).
(Nick Meskell collection)

The Load Haul Years

56 004 and 56 006 arrived in the UK just a month apart in 1977 and today they both sport BR blue livery. 004 - as already documented - has always been blue while 006 passed through the rainbow of colours: blue, Railfreight, Trainload Coal, Load Haul and blue again. Stopping off at Load Haul and what a beauty - 56 006 gleams in the spring sunshine at Tinsley on 12th March 1995. Named only a month earlier, this didn't last long as by August 1999, the loco was undergoing transformation back to BR blue for the September 1999 'Classic Traction' event at the East Lancashire Railway. 56 006 now resides at Barrow Hill. *(Nick Meskell collection)*

Load Haul city Scunthorpe on 20th September 1996 with 56 102 passing on a loaded coal train while a 37 rests against the buffers. Looking at this industrial view, there's no doubt the orange and black was a truly eye-catching livery and a favourite amongst enthusiasts and photographers. The loco was painted in this livery at Brush in Loughborough in January 1996. While in grey with Trainload Coal branding, the loco was named 'Scunthorpe Steel Centenary' in March 1990. Today 56 102 rests at Thornaby. *(Nick Meskell collection)*

Low winter sunshine highlights 56 090 at Healey Mills on 6th December 1997. In total 27 Class 56s received this livery between July 1994 and March 1996 and they were painted at Doncaster Works (21), Crewe Works (4) and Brush Works, Loughborough (2). 56 090 was treated at Doncaster in December 1995. Today, this loco is working in France and is painted in the off-white Fertis livery. *(Nick Meskell collection)*

Some of the locos first painted in Load Haul livery made it into service without the branding: 56 006, 56 034, 56 050, 56 074, 56 077, 56 083, 56 110 and shown here, 56 130 are eight examples known to have missed out on transfers, only to have them applied later. The photo shows a rather naked 56 130 at Knottingley on 22nd January 1995. The loco had only been painted the month before at Doncaster. (See the other 56 130 on page 18). Sadly, this loco was cut up in October 2004. *(Nick Meskell collection)*

The EWS Years

When Wisconsin Central purchased Mainline, Transrail and Load Haul in February 1996, a number of 56s were undergoing works attention and without a 'new' livery as such, they were outshopped in all over white (undercoat/primer). 56 068 was one example and another, shown here was 56 041. Taken at Thornaby on 21st April 1996, the loco sports full yellow ends and small end numerals. Eventually, of course, the loco was painted in the maroon and gold colours with the EW&S branding. *(Nick Meskell collection)*

A lovely shot of 56 088 passing Golf Street (near Carnoustie) on 26th July 1999 with 6A62 tank train from Oxwellmains to Aberdeen Craiginches. This was another of the early repaints, most notable by the different typeface used and of course, the EW&S vice EWS. Another first for this livery was the application of full front end digits. Instead of 088 - the full 56088 has been transferred on in maroon. This practice applied to all classes of loco given EWS colours. This loco survived in service until February 2004 and is now dumped at Thornaby. *(Nick Meskell collection)*

Another early repaint was 56 120, shown here pretty much ex-works at Lincoln on 4th October 1996. During 1996, a total of 12 locos received this early EW&S version: 56 041, 56 051, 56 057, 56 058, 56 059, 56 067, 56 088, 56 089, 56 096, 56 105, 56 114 and 56 120. (The 'other' 56 120 is on page 19). *(Nick Meskell collection)*

The second and final version of the EWS livery wasn't altogether different from the first although it is surprising what difference a typeface makes, even on the cab ends! Looking almost brand new - but actually 16 years old - 56 103 stands at Bescot on 5th July 1997. The loco was named 'STORA' 13 days after this photo was taken at the Stora terminal in Barking. (Stora make cardboard and packaging products). Unlike some, 56 103 enjoyed a varied life with stints at Tinsley, Toton, Stewarts Lane, Motherwell, Cardiff and Immingham. *(Nick Meskell collection)*

Double Headers

Left: A short train for 56 037, comprising of 37 417, one container and one tank. The combination passes Carnoustie on 23rd July 1999 with 6A02 from Mossend Yard to Aberdeen. Note the split grab rail on the front of this loco compared to the full length design carried by most other locos in this book. With the Class 37 fitted with the Blue Star multi working system, these two locos cannot work together although for a train of this size, why would they need to!
(Nick Meskell collection)

Right: The fact that they have 3250hp engines means there aren't many freight trains in the UK that a single loco wouldn't be able to haul and double-heading was never that common. However, all Class 56s were fitted with the Red Diamond multiple working system and over the years they did work in pairs. The photo shows a mixed livery pairing of 56 051+56 126 on 18th July 1998 approaching Millerhill with fly ash/MGR empties outbound from Longannet Power Station. Nine months after this photo was taken, 56 126 was withdrawn after only 16 years in service!
(Nick Meskell collection)

Passenger Trains

Left: Research into the date and train details for this photo have drawn a blank but it's worth including for the novelty value. 56 032 and 47 843 arrive at Coventry on a Virgin Cross Country train. To add to the already unusual sight of this combination, note that 56 032 is without its multiple working cable and there appears to be an additional headlight affixed to the front end grab rail. Closer scrutiny reveals an EWS driver at the controls and a Virgin Trains driver in the secondmans seat. A peeking head in the sixth coach reveals it's not empty stock either!
(Nick Meskell collection)

Right: Always a popular choice for railtours, the Class 56 has a long history of enthusiasts specials running the length and breadth of the country. In this shot 56 081 pauses at Kemble, heading towards Swindon on 23rd November 2002. *(Andy Harkness)*

Final Trains

In their final months, Class 56s were regularly employed on the Plasmor trains to and from Bow. With a third rail, overhead wires and an electricity pylon in view, 56 062 storms though Hackney Wick with 4E25 13.23 Bow to Heck empties on 18th February 2004. *(Justin Perkins)*

A powerful shot of the loaded train, 6L69 the 05.42 Peterborough Yard to Bow on 29th March 2004, also at Hackney Wick. Two days after this photo was taken, 56 078 worked the farewell railtour. *(Justin Perkins)*

The Farewell Tour

Left: Following the decision to take the remaining Class 56s out of service at the end of March 2004, Pathfinder quickly arranged a farewell tour, appropriately named 'The Twilight Grids', on Wednesday 31st. Pictured in the morning mist on the freight only line between Chesterfield and Rotherham, 56 115 storms by with 1Z56, the 05.23 from Bristol Temple Meads to York (via Birmingham New Street, Toton and Doncaster). Note the height of the nameplates on this loco. *(Mary Meskell)*

Right: Upon arrival at York, 56 078 was attached for a mini railtour from York to York via Leeds, Rochdale, Stalybridge and Castleford. Given the headcode 1Z57, running about an hour early and in much better weather, 56 078 shatters the silence at Sherburn-In-Elmet on the last stretch through to York. *(Mary Meskell)*

After a few problems with the multi working and a subsequent one-hour delay, 56 115 blazed the trail on the final journey, 1Z58 from York to Bristol Temple Meads (via Sheffield, Derby, BNS and Worcester Shrub Hill). Pictured at Sherburn-In-Elmet again, sounding good and looking better, 56 115 + 56 078 thunder on by, making history as they pass and bringing the Class 56 story to a close. *(Mary Meskell)*

Gone For Scrap

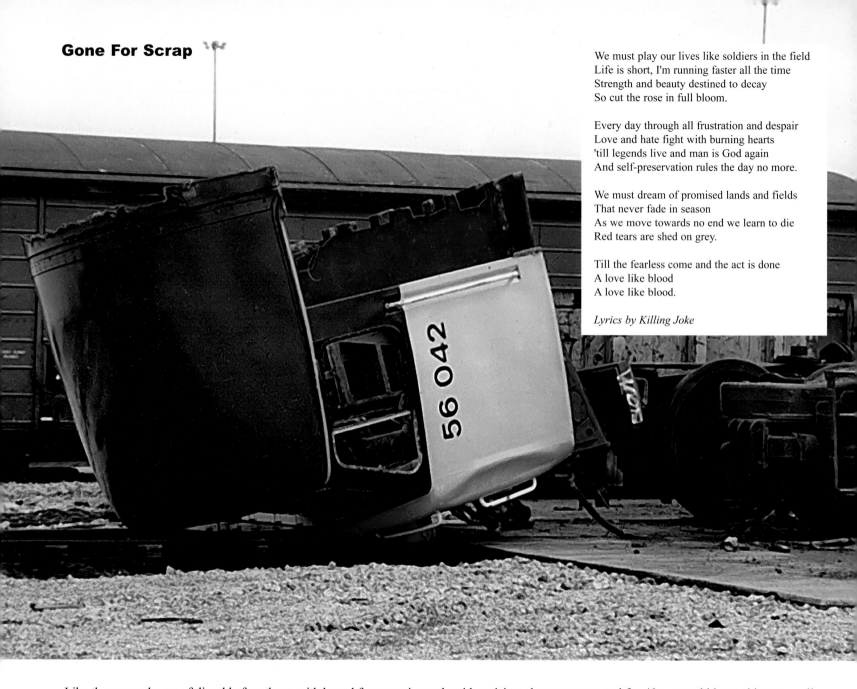

We must play our lives like soldiers in the field
Life is short, I'm running faster all the time
Strength and beauty destined to decay
So cut the rose in full bloom.

Every day through all frustration and despair
Love and hate fight with burning hearts
'till legends live and man is God again
And self-preservation rules the day no more.

We must dream of promised lands and fields
That never fade in season
As we move towards no end we learn to die
Red tears are shed on grey.

Till the fearless come and the act is done
A love like blood
A love like blood.

Lyrics by Killing Joke

Like the many classes of diesel before them, withdrawal from service ends with a visit to the scrap man and for 40+ year old locos this may well be justified. For the Class 56s, having led such short lives, it's odd to see these 'modern' diesels lined up with 08s, 31s, 37s and 47s. Following withdrawal at Toton at the tender age of 12 in September 1991, 56 042 lingered on for three more years before being broken. The cab end lays in the dirt at Toton in this 1994 dated picture. *(Nick Meskell collection)*

Left: Following withdrawal from service in April 1999, 56 080 looks decidedly unhealthy at Wigan in this 10th March 2001 dated photo. Ironically, 13 years earlier this loco was the pride and joy of Yorkshire, when the curtain was pulled back, the applause rang out and 'Selby Coalfield' nameplates were revealed in an October 1989 ceremony at Gascoigne Wood Mine. There was a further twist in the demise of 56 080 after it was sold, moved from Wigan and then scrapped at Cardiff in December 2003.
(Nick Meskell collection)

Right: Taken on the same day as 56 080 above, here is another example of a short lived loco meeting an untimely and cruel end. Still bearing the black diamond coal strip, the sorrowful looking 18 year old 56 126 was completely cut a month after this photo was taken.
(Nick Meskell collection)

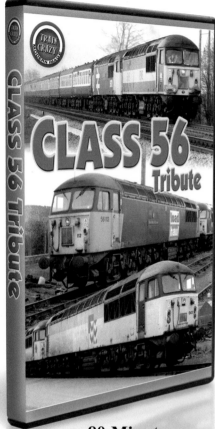
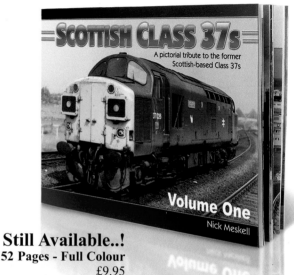